Stop, I Pray

A Guide to Praying
Romans 12
for Your Church

Reign in life
Romans 5:17
Christi Brown

Christi Brown
with Alyssa Brown

Stop, Drop & Pray
A Guide to Praying Romans 12 for Your Church

ISBN: 978-0-578-00282-8

Library of Congress Control Number: 2009903207

Design & layout: Shelley Penninger Roberts
Editor: Karen Schuster Stephens

Printed in the United States of America by InstantPublisher.com

Dedicated
to our church family at
Coronado Baptist Church
and
the Lord Jesus Christ,
the means of God's mercy and grace

Contents

Introduction

I felt the prompting for quite some time before I realized what it was – God calling me out of our Sunday school class. Sitting next to my husband, among dear friends, I listened and laughed and looked up Scriptures along with everyone else. We had been part of this Parents of Teenagers Sunday school class since its inception; I was very happy there. The teacher and his wife are our friends. The fellowship in our class was sweet, and the teaching was God-glorifying and edifying. Why give this up? It did not make sense to me, but the prompting persisted.

One Sunday morning, I rose to pray and be quiet with the Lord before our family's day began. The thought came to me – *Pray. Pray for your church family.* I knew in a moment what my Heavenly Father meant. Once I read an account from the life of Charles Spurgeon, pastor of London's Metropolitan Tabernacle in the mid-to-late 1800's. When visitors came to the church, it was Spurgeon's habit to take them to the basement, to a room where people were always on their knees praying for the church. Spurgeon told them, "Here is the powerhouse for the church." The powerhouse for the church – I had prayed for our church family before, but this was different.

God's direction was clear. Find a quiet place behind the sanctuary and pray during the worship service that follows ours. My heart rejoiced at the thought of 1¼ hours of solid prayer for our church family. I told my husband about it, and he encouraged me to follow God's lead. We went to church and after worship ended, I quietly slipped into the room behind the baptistry. I found just what I was looking for – a closet-sized dressing room where brothers and sisters in Christ prepare for baptism. I went in, closed the door behind me, and breathed a deep sigh. This was my appointed place. I slipped off my shoes, got down on my knees with the Bible open before me, and asked the Lord to show me what to do.

I waited and listened carefully. The worship music began and my mind pictured men, women, young people, and children filing into the sanctuary. Why have they come? I wondered. Are they ready to worship? (Sometimes getting to church is such an ordeal, that once you arrive and collapse into a pew, you feel that you have nothing left to give.) What needs do they have this morning? In what state are their hearts? Who's hurting? Where do I begin?

Praying the Scriptures draws me to my Heavenly Father in a powerful way; it helps turn my mind and heart to Him. So I turned to Romans 12 to follow what was already a familiar pattern of prayer. I listened again, aware that only a wall separated me from the congregation. I raised my hands, placed them on the wall, and began to pray. "O Lord Christ, be exalted in this place. I pray that each one here this morning would know and experience the fullness of Your mercy and grace! May they know how much You love them."

I cannot explain it fully, but a love that is not my own began to pound in my heart. Humbled, I continued to pray one phrase of Romans 12 at a time, listening for the Spirit's impress on my heart to guide further prayer. Before I knew it, the service ended. People were filing out of the sanctuary. God brought me to this quiet place to pray for

His people. It might appear that I served Him; yet He is the One who served me. Prayer is a privilege; it is God's gift to us. I felt a deep satisfaction, combined with a surprising, new love for those for whom I prayed. I felt complete.

Several months have passed. I cannot help but speak of what God gives through this kind of prayer. First comes the gift of stillness. Second is the gift of precious intimacy with the Most High God. Third is the gift of love. As you hold yourself before Him in prayer, He in turn pours Himself into you. His love and mercy fill the nooks and crannies of your heart, and in a marvelous way, His love becomes your own. You begin to love others because He first loved you. Lastly is His gift of purpose. God's plans and purposes replace your own agendas. Priorities change. Passions change. You are changed.

God called me to prayer. He calls you to pray for your church – in the quiet of your home, in the carpool line while you wait for your kids, during your lunch break at work, or at church on Wednesday night or Sunday morning. It is time to *stop…drop…and pray*. You'll be glad you did.

Christi Brown
El Paso, Texas

Why Romans 12?

In approximately 57-58 A.D., the apostle Paul wrote a letter to Christians in Rome. He was in Corinth at the time but was anxious to visit and minister to believers in Rome. His letter, called the book of Romans, might well be called the constitution of the Christian faith. Paul explains the grace of God in its widest implications. The first 11 chapters describe man's desperate need for a Savior and God's merciful provision of salvation by grace, through faith in His Son, the Lord Jesus Christ. In chapter 12 and continuing to the end of the letter, Paul turns to application, urging his brothers in Christ to allow God's grace to transform the way they think and live.

Read Romans 12.

Take time now to read through this remarkable chapter. It helps to know where you are going before you begin the trip.

"Therefore, I urge you, brothers, in view of God's mercy, to offer your bodies as living sacrifices, holy and pleasing to God – this is your spiritual act of worship. Do not conform any longer to the pattern of this world, but be transformed by the renewing of your mind. Then you will be able to test and approve what God's will is – His good, pleasing and perfect will.

For by the grace given me I say to every one of you: Do not think of yourself more highly than you ought, but rather think of yourself with sober judgment, in accordance with the measure of faith God has given you. Just as each of us has one body with many members, and these members do not all have the same function, so in Christ we who are many form one body, and each member belongs to all the others. We have different gifts, according to the grace given us. If a man's gift is prophesying, let him use it in proportion to his faith. If it is serving, let him serve; if it is teaching, let him teach; if it is encouraging, let him encourage; if it is contributing to the needs of others, let him give generously; if it is leadership, let him govern diligently; if it is showing mercy, let him do it cheerfully.

Love must be sincere. Hate what is evil; cling to what is good. Be devoted to one another in brotherly love. Honor one another above yourselves. Never be lacking in zeal, but keep your spiritual fervor, serving the Lord. Be joyful in hope, patient in affliction, faithful in prayer. Share with God's people who are in need. Practice hospitality.

Bless those who persecute you; bless and do not curse. Rejoice with those who rejoice; mourn with those who mourn. Live in harmony with one another. Do not be proud, but be willing to associate with people of low position. Do not be conceited.

Do not repay anyone evil for evil. Be careful to do what is right in the eyes of everybody. If it is possible, as far as it depends on you, live at peace with everyone. Do not take revenge, my friends, but leave room for God's wrath, for it is written: 'It is mine to avenge; I will repay,' says the Lord.

On the contrary:

> *'If your enemy is hungry, feed him;*
> *if he is thirsty, give him something to*
> *drink. In doing this, you will heap*
> *burning coals on his head.'*

Do not be overcome by evil, but overcome evil with good."

For the purpose of this devotional guide to prayer, we divided the text of Romans 12 into 30 selections – one for each day of the month. Use it as a tool and not as a rigid guide.

Remember that the apostle Paul wrote these words to encourage Christians to live out their faith. Ask the Lord to make the words come alive for you. Pray each Romans 12 selection aloud slowly. Then be still and listen. It is the Holy Spirit's work to take the words of Scripture and apply them to the heart. How do these words from Romans 12 speak to your heart and set of circumstances? What needs in your church does this particular part of Scripture address? Our prayers, written in response to each selection, are included to help you begin. Pray them aloud to God just as they are written. Write your personal thoughts and prayers on the lines provided.

Other verses from Scripture are added to broaden and enhance your prayer. Many of these are personalized so that you can easily pray them back to God. Ask Him, "How does this apply, or what does this look like in my life or in the life of my church?" Then be still and listen. Write down specific thoughts, prayers, and perhaps even the names of people that come to mind.

Day 1

"Therefore, I urge you, brothers, in view of God's mercy...
(Romans 12:1a)

Most High and Holy God, be exalted in our church. Enlarge our view of You and our understanding of the depths of Your mercy and grace to us in the Lord Jesus Christ. Not one of us deserves or merits Your attention and favor. Cause us to be astonished at all You have done for us in Christ. Make us feel our debt to You.

Author's note: Record your own prayers and your thoughts about God's mercy on the lines that follow.

Lord, cause each of us to "...grow in the grace and knowledge of our Lord and Savior Jesus Christ" (2 Peter 3:18). What steps must I take to grow in grace and knowledge?

_____

_____

_____

_____

_____

_____

_____

_____

May we yearn for the *much more* of the Christian life. "For if, by the trespass of the one man, death reigned through that one man, how much more will those who receive God's abundant provision of grace and of the gift of righteousness reign in life through the one man, Jesus Christ" (Romans 5:17). May we be Christians who reign in life through Jesus Christ!

_____

_____

_____

_____

_____

_____

_____

_____

_____

Lord, I pray for the unsaved men, women, young people, and children who pass through our church doors every week. Open their eyes and turn them from darkness to light. Soften their hearts; convict them of sin and of their need for You. Reveal Yourself to them as " '...The Lord, the Lord, the compassionate and gracious God, slow to anger, abounding in love and faithfulness, maintaining love to thousands, and forgiving wickedness, rebellion and sin. Yet [You do] not leave the guilty unpunished...' " (Exodus 34:6-7a).

May lost souls hear the gospel, the glorious news of salvation by grace, through faith in Jesus Christ! Bring them to salvation and a personal knowledge of Your mercy and grace.

Help our church to be a welcoming place. Empower us, by Your Holy Spirit, to show genuine warmth and love to those who visit. What can I do to make our church more welcoming?

_____

_____

_____

_____

_____

_____

_____

_____

_____

_____

_____

Lord, is my faith attractive? Do others want what I have? Make my faith winsome and appealing so that it draws others to Christ, like "bees to honey."

_____

_____

_____

_____

_____

_____

_____

_____

_____

_____

_____

Day 2

to offer your bodies as living sacrifices, holy and pleasing to God… (Romans 12:1b)

Lord, how can we ever thank You for all that You have done for us in Christ? Your mercy gives us the privilege of offering ourselves to You. May our sense of debt be such that we willingly offer our bodies, our very lives to You. We confess that this giving of ourselves is hard. It means giving up control and surrendering our so-called rights. It means serving You rather than serving ourselves. It is easy to give our money and our time. But sacrifice means death – dying to our old lives and selfish ways. Why do I resist? What keeps me from this kind of surrender?

Lord, You do not want our stuff – You want us. You want each of us to willingly give You our minds, thoughts, hearts, affections, emotions, eyes, mouths, hands, and feet. This is dying to ourselves; it ushers in a freedom and abundance that satisfies in life as nothing else can. This is what we were made for. This is the only kind of life that pleases You. It is only through Christ that we can be holy and pleasing to You. Apart from Him, we are nothing and have nothing to give. Lord, what area(s) of my life am I holding back? Why am I afraid of giving You control?

Lord, You called us to this sacrifice when You told Your disciples, "...If anyone would come after Me, he must deny himself and take up his cross and follow Me. For whoever wants to save his life will lose it, but whoever loses his life for Me will find it" (Matthew 16:24-25).

_____

_____

_____

_____

_____

_____

_____

_____

_____

Lord, this sacrifice is the reasonable response to the mercy and grace extended to us in Christ. It is not something we have to do; it is something we should want to do. As the fire of heaven consumed animal sacrifices in the Old Testament, may Your Spirit consume and use us for Your glory.

_____

_____

_____

_____

_____

_____

_____

_____

_____

_____

_____

Lord, what can I do today for Your kingdom?

Day 3

this is your spiritual act of worship (Romans 12:1c).

Worship is *"worthship"*. It is the feeling and expression of praise for You, Lord! It is the act of ascribing glory to Your name, and it is the proper response to You. I bow before You today and praise You as Sovereign Ruler over all things. I praise You for Your holiness, Your majesty, and splendor. I praise You for…

_____

_____

_____

_____

_____

_____

_____

_____

_____

_____

_____

_____

_____

_____

_____

_____

_____

_____

_____

This offering of ourselves is done only through the power of the indwelling Holy Spirit. Your Spirit compels us to make this sacrifice. Accept our lives, O Lord, as offerings of reverence for You and devotion to You. You alone are worthy. You are Most High and Merciful God. We are Your debtors and owe You our lives.

Day 4

Do not conform any longer to the pattern of this world...
(Romans 12:2a)

Lord, help us to stop being conformed to the world and its ways. Forgive us that often our lives do not look any different from the lives of unbelievers around us. Convict us of worldliness – of specific ways in which we adopt worldly thinking and behavior that water down our witness for Christ.

Examine our thoughts, words, and actions and bring to light all that is not of You. "Search me, O God, and know my heart; test me and know my anxious thoughts. See if there is any offensive way in me, and lead me in the way everlasting" (Psalm 139:23-24).

Let us hear and apply the apostle Paul's words to our own lives. "You were taught, with regard to your former way of life, to put off your old self, which is being corrupted by its deceitful desires; to be made new in the attitude of your minds; and to put on the new self, created to be like God in true righteousness and holiness" (Ephesians 4:22-24). What specific attitudes and behaviors must I, by the Holy Spirit's power, put off? What attitudes and behaviors must I put on?

Day 5

*but be transformed by the renewing of your mind
(Romans 12:2b).*

O Lord, transform us. Literally change our character
from the inside out, by the renewing of our minds. Speak
to us through Your Word and through Your Holy Spirit.
Renew our minds each time we encounter Your Word –
in personal Bible study, in Sunday school, or as we listen
to a sermon. Cause our thoughts to line up with Your
thoughts.

Guide this process, as we shift from worldly thinking to
God-centered thinking. May Your Word become the lens
through which we view everything.

As You change the way we think, change the way we live. *Christ in us* means we are different. We are no longer mastered by sin – we are mastered by Christ. Galatians 2:20 is true of each of us, "I have been crucified with Christ and I no longer live, but Christ lives in me. The life I live in the body, I live by faith in the Son of God, Who loved me and gave Himself for me."

Lord, Your power is at work within each one of us. We are *salt* and *light* in our homes, offices, schools, neighborhoods, communities, towns, cities, and nations. Use each one of us to penetrate and influence the culture (Matthew 5:13-16).

Make us living testimonies to the fact that the gospel of Jesus Christ is relevant to every area of life in the 21st century. Lord, help me to identify the circles of influence in my life and to be purposeful in my witness for Christ.

Forgive my hesitation and tentativeness in speaking to others about You. Remind us of Christ's promise to each member of His body, "But you will receive power when the Holy Spirit comes on you; and you will be My witnesses in Jerusalem, and in all Judea and Samaria, and to the ends of the earth" (Acts 1:8).

Lord, we are Your witnesses. Empower and embolden us. I am Your witness. Give me courage and specific opportunities to tell others how wonderful You are.

_____

_____

_____

_____

_____

_____

_____

_____

_____

I pray "...that [we] may be active in sharing [our] faith, so that [we] will have a full understanding of every good thing we have in Christ" (Philemon 6). Lord, each time I tell someone else about You, it deepens my understanding of Your grace, and my love for You grows.

_____

_____

_____

_____

Lord, to whom shall I witness today? Who is it that needs to hear of Your mercy and grace? Put names on my heart and people in my path.

_____

_____

_____

_____

_____

_____

_____

_____

_____

_____

_____

_____

_____

_____

_____

_____

_____

_____

_____

_____

_____

_____

_____

_____

_____

Day 6

Then you will be able to test and approve what God's will is – His good, pleasing and perfect will (Romans 12:2c).

Lord, Your will is that each of us be conformed to the image of Christ. As we become more like Him, we increasingly desire Your will for our lives rather than our own will. We begin to want what You want. The more we desire Your will for our lives, the clearer Your path will be.

O Lord, mold our wills to Your will. Identify areas where my life is out of step with Your will. Make the way clear.

Help each one of us to discover that Your will for us is good; it cannot be otherwise because You are good, and You love us perfectly. There is nothing that touches our lives that You will not use for our good. Period. Lord, help us look for the eternal good in everything.

Mature us so that we learn that Your will is pleasing – Your will satisfies and fulfills as nothing else can. Even trouble and sorrow, painful as they may be, serve Your purposes. They create need in us, but Your grace is sufficient for our every need. Your grace stabilizes, steadies, strengthens, and even satisfies. Lord, I need Your grace to change my attitude toward these specific circumstances in my life...

Day 7

For by the grace given me I say to every one of you: Do not think of yourself more highly than you ought, but rather think of yourself with sober judgment, in accordance with the measure of faith God has given you (Romans 12:3).

O Lord, help us think rightly of ourselves. Give us a Biblical self-image. How tragic when we think too highly of ourselves, of our place in the body of Christ, and the spiritual gifts that we have been given. It is also tragic to think too little of ourselves, of our value to the body of Christ, and of the gifts that we have been given. Both scenarios cripple us and prevent us from being effective members of the body. How do I view myself and the place You have given me in the body of Christ? How do I view others?

Help us look at our brothers and sisters in Christ and remember that each of us is reconciled to You through the blood of Your Son, Jesus Christ. Each member of Your body is chosen by You and precious. Each is a child of Yours, adopted into Your family and made an heir with Christ.

Christ's image is being formed in the other members of His body, just as His image is being formed in me. We are on our way to glory. Together. What must I do to align my thinking with Your Word?

Convict us of pride. It puffs up and inflates our view of ourselves. People who are puffed up cannot get close to others. Pride keeps us from engaging, loving, and serving one another. Lord, humble me. Humble us. Do not let pride keep us from serving Your kingdom; don't let it tear our church apart.

On the other hand, keep us from thinking too little of ourselves, of who we are in Christ and the role we play within His body. Feelings of inadequacy often reveal a focus on self rather than Christ. Forgive us, Lord. Help us to honestly assess our strengths and weaknesses. Put us where You want us. Use us as You will, by the power of Your Spirit and for the glory of Your name. As Paul writes, "Not that we are competent in ourselves to claim anything for ourselves, but our competence comes from God" (2 Corinthians 3:5).

Day 8

Just as each of us has one body with many members, and these members do not all have the same function, so in Christ we who are many form one body, and each member belongs to all the others (Romans 12:4-5).

We are one body. You made us into a living, breathing organism – we are one body whether we feel like it or not. Each of us belongs *first* to Christ and then to one another. To what degree do I view the body of Christ in this way?

Individually and corporately, we are to live "to the praise of Your glorious grace, which You [have] freely given us in the One You [love]" (Ephesians 1:6). O Father, what would it look like for me and for our church family to live to the praise of Your glorious grace?

_____

_____

_____

_____

_____

_____

_____

_____

Each of us has a unique part to play in the functioning of Christ's body. We have distinct roles to fill, and the health and integrity of the body depend on our fulfilling these individual roles. It is similar to the human body, which cannot function properly without all of its parts. Each part plays a unique role. The hand cannot do everything; it has its function and cannot serve as a liver, an eye, a foot, or a kneecap. O Lord, help me to appreciate the unique role that each of my brothers and sisters in Christ has in Your body.

_____

_____

_____

_____

_____

I pray for those who think that church is the building in which we meet. I pray for those who think of church as little more than a social club. I pray for those who feel that the Pastor *is* the church. Bind us together with the truth that the local church is a body of believers, a family joined together with Christ Jesus as its head.

I pray for those who feel that corporate worship is either an option or an obligation. May they begin "…to grasp how wide and long and high and deep is the love of Christ…" (Ephesians 3:18). Bring them to worship. Surprise them. Reveal Yourself to them through the men, women, young people, and children who worship at their sides. May they rejoice to come to the house of the Lord!

Lord, I pray for those who do not feel connected to our church family. They come in quietly for worship, sit in the back, and slip out the door without so much as a hug or a hello. I pray for those who wonder, "Does anyone even know that I am here?" Cause them to realize that the best way to connect with others is by extending themselves. Make us willing to take the first step and to look for ways to pour ourselves into the lives of others.

Day 9

We have different gifts, according to the grace given us (Romans 12:6a).

Lord, help each member of my church family to identify his or her spiritual gifts. Remind us that Jesus gives us these gifts. They are His grace to us. We do not deserve or earn them. Thank You, Lord Jesus, for the gift(s) You have given me.

Author's note: Talk with your Pastor if you have not already identified your own spiritual gift(s).

_____

_____

_____

_____

Keep us from the prideful mentality that says, "Because I'm a better person or a more important Christian, I received the gift I did." Some gifts are more visible, like preaching, teaching, and leadership. But these gifts are no more significant to the good of the whole body than the gifts of serving, encouragement, giving, or showing mercy.

_____

_____

_____

_____

Spiritual gifts are not reasons for pride. They are *grace gifts* given for the building up of the body. They are not for our own edification, but for the edification of others. Spiritual gifts are given in the context of the body of Christ and are not about us at all.

_____

_____

_____

_____

_____

_____

_____

_____

Gifts are given "to prepare God's people for works of service, so that the body of Christ may be built up until we all reach unity in the faith and in the knowledge of the Son of God and become mature, attaining to the whole measure of the fullness of Christ" (Ephesians 4:12-13). Lord, how can I use my gift(s) to build up the body of Christ?

_____

_____

_____

_____

_____

_____

_____

_____

Day 10

If a man's gift is prophesying, let him use it in proportion to his faith. If it is serving, let him serve; if it is teaching, let him teach; if it is encouraging, let him encourage; if it is contributing to the needs of others, let him give generously; if it is leadership, let him govern diligently; if it is showing mercy, let him do it cheerfully (Romans 12:6b-8).

Lord, teach me to value the gifts given to each member of our church family. Help me to recognize the individuals who have the gifts named in this passage, so that I can write their names down and pray for them accordingly. I rejoice to see brothers and sisters step out in faith and use their gifts for the building up of the body. May we strengthen and encourage each other.

Preachers – May those who have been given the ability to set forth and explain the Scriptures hunger and thirst for Your Word. Make Scripture alive, fresh, and relevant to them each day. Give them wisdom and direction in its meaning and application. Give them courage and the ability to speak the truth in love.

May they "Preach the Word; be prepared in season and out of season; correct, rebuke and encourage – with great patience and careful instruction" (2 Timothy 4:2).

May they "…[speak] to men for their strengthening, encouragement and comfort" (1 Corinthians 14:3). May their words be "...a demonstration of the Spirit's power, so that [our] faith might not rest on men's wisdom, but on God's power" (1 Corinthians 2:4b-5).

May they never be "...ashamed of the gospel, because it is the power of God for the salvation of everyone who believes: first for the Jew, then for the Gentile" (Romans 1:16).

Preachers

Servants – I pray for those who whose ministry is service, those who are *helpers* in every sense of the word. They step up, no matter how large or small the task. These are the people who make it possible for the rest of us to exercise our gifts.

May they not grow weary in service. May their labors bear much fruit. Give them joy in serving. May they "...not become weary in doing good, for at the proper time [they] will reap a harvest if [they] do not give up. Therefore, as [they] have opportunity, let [them] do good to all people, especially to those who belong to the family of believers" (Galatians 6:9-10).

May they serve in and through the power of Your Holy Spirit. "If anyone serves, he should do it with the strength God provides, so that in all things God may be praised through Jesus Christ" (1 Peter 4:11b).

Lord, strengthen these servants with the promise that "[You are] not unjust; [You] will not forget [their] work and the love [they] have shown [You] as [they] have helped [Your] people and continue to help them" (Hebrews 6:10).

Servants

Teachers – O Lord, these members of the body love to learn and get a thrill out of teaching others what they have learned. Protect their preparation and Bible study time. "Open [their] eyes that [they] may see wonderful things in Your law" (Psalm 119:18).

Give our teachers understanding of Your Word and direction in its application. Remind them that "...[You] give wisdom, and from [Your] mouth come knowledge and understanding" (Proverbs 2:6).

May they "...teach what is in accord with sound doctrine" (Titus 2:1).

May each one, "In [their] teaching show integrity, seriousness and soundness of speech that cannot be condemned..." (Titus 2:7b-8a).

God, You are *Elohim*, the Creator of the ends of the earth. Give our teachers energy, enthusiasm, and creativity. Give them insight into the hearts and minds of those they teach. Encourage them by making us eager and conscientious students.

Teachers

Encouragers – These are the people who come alongside to give comfort, courage, and hope. They embolden and lift us up. They are a source of *spiritual steel* for those around them. Lord, keep these precious ones close to You. Feed them through Your Word. Strengthen them so that they are able to speak truth into the lives of others.

May their lives and ministries remind us that "...great is Your love, reaching to the heavens; Your faithfulness reaches to the skies" (Psalm 57:10).

May Your Spirit fill them with "...love, joy, peace, patience, kindness, goodness, faithfulness, gentleness and self-control" (Galatians 5:22-23a).

Encouragers are people who make time to write the notes, make the phone calls, bake the pies, send the flowers, and set the coffee or lunch dates that most of us never get around to doing. Lord, give them eyes to see the weary and discouraged. Give them hearts of compassion.

Encouragers

Givers – Help me to pray for those who contribute and give generously to the needs of the body. You put resources into their hands because You know they can be counted on to give them away as You direct. They give freely; no strings attached. They know that what they give away is not theirs in the first place. Bring needs to their attention. Give them courage to trust You as they give generously and obediently to help others.

May they find that "…[You] will meet all [their] needs according to [Your] glorious riches in Christ Jesus" (Philippians 4:19).

May they "…not become weary in doing good, for at the proper time [they] will reap a harvest if [they] do not give up. Therefore, as [they] have opportunity, let [them] do good to all people, especially to those who belong to the family of believers" (Galatians 6:9-10).

May each one give "…what he has decided in his heart to give, not reluctantly or under compulsion, for God loves a cheerful giver" (2 Corinthians 9:7).

Givers

Leaders – We thank You, Lord, for those who are called to govern and lead our church. Help us to hold them in high regard in love. Please shepherd them as they shepherd us. Give them wisdom, diligence, and courage. Give them love for those they lead.

May they be God-pleasers rather than man-pleasers – church leaders who "…are not trying to please men but God, who tests [their] hearts" (1 Thessalonians 2:4b).

Help them to "…flee from all this [love of money], and pursue righteousness, godliness, faith, love, endurance and gentleness." May they "Fight the good fight of the faith" (1Timothy 6:11-12a).

May Your grace and power rest on our church leaders. I pray they experience the truth that "…[You] did not give [them] a spirit of timidity, but a spirit of power, of love and of self-discipline" (2 Timothy 1:7).

Help them "…guard what has been entrusted to [their] care" (1Timothy 6:20a).

Encourage them with the reminder that "…when the Chief Shepherd appears, [they] will receive the crown of glory that will never fade away" (1 Peter 5:4).

Leaders

Merciful – Give joy to those who have the gift of mercy. These are the people whose hearts have been deepened and refined by Your mercy and as such, they have a special love and compassion for others. They listen and love without judging. They are rich in mercy because You worked it into their hearts.

Remind them that God's people are called "To act justly and to love mercy and to walk humbly with [their] God" (Micah 6:8b).

May Your Holy Spirit give them heavenly wisdom that "...is first of all pure; then peace-loving, considerate, submissive, full of mercy and good fruit, impartial and sincere" (James 3:17).

Give them Your eyes. Give them Your words. Give them Your love – love that is patient and kind; love that "...does not envy, it does not boast, it is not proud. It is not rude, it is not self-seeking, it is not easily angered, it keeps no record of wrongs" (1 Corinthians 13:4b-5). Give them a love that "...does not delight in evil but rejoices with the truth. It always protects, always trusts, always hopes, always perseveres" (1 Corinthians 13:6-7).

Merciful

Lord, help me to pray for those who preach, serve, teach, encourage, give, lead, and show mercy. Please give me specific opportunities to encourage them as well.

Day 11

Love must be sincere (Romans 12:9a).

Love others through us, Holy Spirit. We cannot love one another apart from Your work in our hearts. Lord, You have "…poured out [Your] love into our hearts by the Holy Spirit, whom [You have] given us" (Romans 5:5b). Cause us to love one another as You have loved us.

_____

_____

_____

_____

_____

_____

_____

Train us to "Be imitators of God, therefore, as dearly loved children and live a life of love, just as Christ loved us and gave Himself up for us as a fragrant offering and sacrifice to God" (Ephesians 5:1-2). This kind of love is not a feeling; it is a sacrificial commitment to care for and serve one another. I want to imitate You, O Christ.

_____

_____

_____

_____

_____

_____

Teach us to love sincerely – to be genuine and constant in our love for one another. Help us to put away our masks and be real. Make us transparent and vulnerable. Prompt us to "Be kind and compassionate to one another, forgiving each other, just as in Christ [You] forgave [us]" (Ephesians 4:32).

Day 12

Hate what is evil… (Romans 12:9b)

Holy God, cause us to hate what is evil – to hate the injurious, the harmful, the offensive, and that which causes ruin or destruction. "Let those who love the Lord hate evil…" (Psalm 97:10a).

Give us a healthy hatred of sin. We are to "…count [ourselves] dead to sin but alive to God in Christ Jesus" (Romans 6:11). Sin no longer reigns in us. Help us to shun it, flee it, and to hold one another accountable for it. Lord, make me cold-blooded about sin in my life. I want to take sin as seriously as You do.

Lord, search our hearts. Reveal sin. We praise and thank You that "If we confess our sins, [You are] faithful and just and will forgive us our sins and purify us from all unrighteousness" (1 John 1:9). Make us quick to confess. O Christ, hide us in Your wounds, and purify us with Your blood. Restore us.

Strengthen my brothers and sisters who face temptation today. Help them to remember that Your sons and daughters are no longer slaves to sin.

Lord, may they experience the truth that "No temptation has seized [them] except what is common to man. And [You are] faithful; [You] will not let [them] be tempted beyond what [they] can bear. But when [they] are tempted, [You] will also provide a way out so that [they] can stand up under it" (1 Corinthians 10:13). Show them Your way of escape, and give them victory.

Day 13

cling to what is good (Romans 12:9c).

O Lord, cause us to cling to what is good. You are good –
consistently, constantly, continuously good. Keep us close
by Your side. Embed Your Word into our hearts.

Thank You that "Your word is a lamp to [our] feet and a
light for [our] path" (Psalm 119:105).

"I have hidden Your word in my heart that I might not sin
against You" (Psalm 119:11).

_____

_____

_____

_____

_____

_____

Strengthen us, by the power of Your Holy Spirit, to stand
upon Your Word day by day and choice by choice.

_____

_____

_____

_____

_____

_____

_____

Teach us to say "...'No' to ungodliness and worldly passions, and to live self-controlled, upright and godly lives in this present age, while we wait for the blessed hope – the glorious appearing of our great God and Savior, Jesus Christ, who gave Himself for us to redeem us from all wickedness and to purify for Himself a people that are His very own, eager to do what is good" (Titus 2:12-14). Lord, I am eager to do what is good. Where do You see ungodliness and worldly passions in my life? Where do I need to say "NO"?

Day 14

Be devoted to one another in brotherly love (Romans 12:10a).

Help us be devoted to one another – to be loyal and faithful and to think nothing of going the extra mile. In what ways do I fail to show loyalty and faithfulness to others in our church family? Show me, Lord.

_____

_____

_____

_____

_____

_____

_____

_____

Keep us from getting so caught up in the business and busyness of church that we miss seeing a brother or sister in need. We're family! We are to love and care for one another in a way that makes unbelievers marvel.

_____

_____

_____

_____

_____

_____

_____

_____

Cause us to move beyond our circle of friends and comfort zones. Help us to extend ourselves to people who do not look like we look or dress like we dress, but nonetheless are our brothers and sisters in Christ.

What can I do today to show brotherly love for someone in my church family?

Day 15

Honor one another above yourselves (Romans 12:10b).

O Father, humble us, and humble me! Church is not about having my felt needs met. It is about worshipping You and equipping Your people to serve Your kingdom.

O Lord, I look around the sanctuary. Each individual is created in Your image and deserves respect and honor. I am no better or worse than they. We are all broken people, made whole through the precious blood of Jesus Christ and the sanctifying work of the Holy Spirit. Give me Your eyes to see others as image-bearers of Christ.

Forgive our selfish ambition and vain conceit. May we count it a privilege to honor one another above ourselves. Whom can I serve and honor today?

Day 16

Never be lacking in zeal, but keep your spiritual fervor, serving the Lord (Romans 12:11).

Set us on fire, Holy Spirit. Cause us to burn for Jesus Christ. Make us an impassioned church body, one that is set apart and sold out for Christ's sake. May our zeal be grounded in truth and love. May everything we do serve Christ's glory and Christ's kingdom.

Lord, "The hour has come for [us] to wake up from [our] slumber, because our salvation is nearer now than when we first believed. The night is nearly over; the day is almost here. So let us put aside the deeds of darkness and put on the armor of light" (Romans 13:11b-12). Wake up, church! Time is short.

Lord Jesus, preparing for Your return does not mean packing our bags and sitting at the end of the driveway. It means waking up every morning with a sense of anticipation. It means listening for Your voice in Your Word and following the slightest promptings of Your Spirit.

Lord, show me how to make this day count for Your kingdom.

Day 17

Be joyful in hope... (Romans 12:12a)

Lord, make us joy-filled people. The hope we have in Jesus Christ is a sure and certain hope – not a cross your fingers, make a wish kind of hope. It is the promise of eternal life – a promise made by God the Father, secured by God the Son, and sealed by God the Holy Spirit. It is a promise that those who are cleansed by the blood of Christ and sanctified by the work of His Spirit will one day be glorified in Christ. *Hallelujah!*

Open the eyes of our hearts so that we may know the hope to which You called us in Christ. We don't just want to know it intellectually; we want to daily experience the fullness of this marvelous hope. "May the God of hope fill [us] with all joy and peace as [we] trust in Him, so that [we] may overflow with hope by the power of the Holy Spirit" (Romans 15:13).

Lord, may Your mercy and grace cause our hearts to sing. "Praise be to the Lord, for He has heard my cry for mercy. The Lord is my strength and my shield; my heart trusts in Him, and I am helped. My heart leaps for joy and I will give thanks to Him in song" (Psalm 28:6-7).

Even when hard times come and smiles are wiped from our faces, help us cling to our hope in Christ. "When I said, 'My foot is slipping,' Your love, O Lord, supported me. When anxiety was great within me, Your consolation brought joy to my soul" (Psalm 94:18-19).

I pray for those who are suffering. Shepherd them. Comfort and quiet them. Make them lie down in the green pastures of Your Word; lead them beside the quiet waters of Your Spirit's presence. Be the *lifter* of their heads, the *soother* of their hearts. Give them joy that surpasses their pain.

Day 18

patient in affliction… (Romans 12:12b)

Father, when darkness comes, our tendency is to turn inward, focusing on ourselves and longing for deliverance. Help us remember that our darkness is as light to You. You are the eternal, omniscient God. Your ways are perfect and blameless. It is never wrong to trust You. Teach us, instead, to long for You and to wait quietly for the unfolding of Your will. Produce the fruit of patience in our lives.

No matter the winds that blow and howl around me, I belong to You, and that is enough. With the Psalmist I cry, "Why are you downcast, O my soul? Why so disturbed within me? Put your hope in God, for I will yet praise Him, my Savior and my God" (Psalm 43:5).

"I waited patiently for the Lord; He turned to me and heard my cry. He lifted me out of the slimy pit, out of the mud and mire; He set my feet on a rock and gave me a firm place to stand. He put a new song in my mouth, a hymn of praise to our God" (Psalm 40:1-3a). Lord, give me a new song.

Give us eyes to see those in our church family who hurt. Break our hearts with the things that break their hearts. Help us to come alongside them as they wait for darkness to lift. Give us the privilege of strengthening one another in the Lord.

Lord, show me the people who carry heavy burdens so that I can help bear the load.

_____

_____

_____

_____

_____

_____

_____

_____

_____

_____

_____

_____

_____

_____

_____

_____

_____

_____

_____

_____

_____

_____

_____

_____

_____

_____

_____

Day 19

faithful in prayer (Romans 12:12c).

Forgive our prayerlessness.

_____

_____

_____

_____

_____

_____

_____

_____

_____

_____

We are grateful for the privilege of approaching You, Father, through the blood of Your Son, Jesus Christ. "For we do not have a high priest who is unable to sympathize with our weaknesses, but we have One who has been tempted in every way, just as we are – yet was without sin. Let us then approach the throne of grace with confidence, so that we may receive mercy and find grace to help us in our time of need" (Hebrews 4:15-16).

_____

_____

_____

_____

_____

_____

_____

Make our church a "praying church." Give us a hunger and a thirst for time alone with You. Teach us to listen for Your voice in Your Word and through Your Spirit. Teach us to talk with You like a child quietly talks with his mother or father before bed at night – vulnerable, transparent, and trusting.

_____
_____
_____
_____
_____
_____
_____
_____

Cause us to care for each other. Help us to be vulnerable and transparent with one another. Make our church a place where it is okay to be fragile and to admit weakness and need. Lord, how approachable am I? Do people feel that they can be transparent with me?

_____
_____
_____
_____
_____
_____
_____
_____

Lord, it is a great privilege to pray *with* and *for* a brother or sister in Christ. Bind our hearts together through prayer. Teach me to write down my prayers so that I can go back and see evidence of Your faithfulness to answer them.

May answered prayer be cause for great delight and thanksgiving in our church family!

Day 20

Share with God's people who are in need (Romans 12:13a).

O God, give us courage to express our needs. Give us grace to accept the help that our brothers and sisters in Christ offer to us. Give us eyes to see the needs of others. Help us hold loosely to what we have been given and be obedient to share as You lead. This is brotherly love.

"If anyone has material possessions and sees his brother in need but has no pity on him, how can the love of God be in him? Dear children, let us not love with words or tongue but with actions and in truth" (1 John 3:17-18). Lord, help me to put my money where my mouth is.

Day 21

Practice hospitality (Romans 12:13b).

Lord, help us to practice hospitality at church. This is our *church home* – may we be gracious and welcoming to all who enter its doors. It can be intimidating to visit a church. Help me recognize visitors and be quick to greet them and do whatever is necessary to make them feel at home.

Cause us to practice hospitality in our homes as well. The most beautifully appointed home is not always the most hospitable. What makes a place welcoming is the kindness and love expressed there. May each of us, no matter what kind of home we have, count it a privilege to open our door to someone else in the name of Christ. Help us show kindness and love to those who have no opportunity to repay us.

Day 22

Bless those who persecute you; bless and do not curse (Romans 12:14).

Lord, forgive me when I do not want to bless those who oppose or persecute me; I don't even want to be nice to them. Why should I? They don't deserve it.

But then, I don't deserve the mercy and kindness You have shown me. O God, forgive me. Who am I to refuse forgiveness?

_____

_____

_____

_____

_____

_____

_____

_____

_____

_____

_____

_____

_____

_____

_____

_____

For He whom we serve "...was oppressed and afflicted, yet He did not open His mouth; He was led like a lamb to the slaughter, and as a sheep before her shearers is silent, so He did not open His mouth" (Isaiah 53:7).

His cry, as they nailed Him to the cross was, "...Father, forgive them, for they do not know what they are doing" (Luke 23:34). Lord Jesus, Your love humbles me.

Lord, You never put us in a place where we cannot give You glory. Give us victory even now. Be glorified through our lives. Help us refuse the temptation to retaliate. Help us choose to bless others instead.

I pray for my brothers and sisters who face opposition and even persecution. Hide Your promises in their hearts. Protect them. Surround them with favor as with a shield. May they discover that "The eternal God is [their] refuge, and underneath are the everlasting arms" (Deuteronomy 33:27a).

"So do not fear, for I am with you; do not be dismayed, for I am your God. I will strengthen you and help you; I will uphold you with My righteous right hand" (Isaiah 41:10). Lord, reveal Yourself to them.

Day 23

Rejoice with those who rejoice… (Romans 12:15a)

"Rejoice in the Lord always. I will say it again: Rejoice!" (Philippians 4:4). O Lord, Your greatness and mercy are reasons for rejoicing.

"I will exalt You, my God the King; I will praise Your name for ever and ever. Every day I will praise You and extol Your name for ever and ever. Great [are You] Lord and most worthy of praise; [Your] greatness no one can fathom. One generation will commend Your works to another; they will tell of Your mighty acts. They will speak of the glorious splendor of Your majesty, and I will meditate on Your wonderful works. They will tell of the power of Your awesome works, and I will proclaim Your great deeds. They will celebrate Your abundant goodness and joyfully sing of Your righteousness" (Psalm 145:1-7).

Lord, we want to be a church family where joys are shared and multiplied. Help us to celebrate one another's blessings and victories.

_____

_____

_____

_____

_____

_____

_____

_____

How do I respond when Your blessings are poured into someone else's life? "Search me, O God, and know my heart; test me and know my anxious thoughts. See if there is any offensive way in me, and lead me in the way everlasting" (Psalm 139:23-24). Lord, search my heart and reveal envy, jealousy, and resentment that lead to bitterness and keep me from rejoicing for others.

_____

_____

_____

_____

_____

_____

_____

_____

_____

Day 24

mourn with those who mourn (Romans 12:15b).

Make us willing to come alongside those who mourn. We do not need to have all the answers for their questions. It is not up to us to ease their pain. We are simply to love them to You, Jesus. We need to be there for them – to listen, take them in our arms, and serve them in whatever ways You lead us. Help us point them, gently and lovingly, to You; for You hold them in Your hands and love them perfectly.

May those who mourn experience the rich reality of Your presence. May they testify that, "Even though [they] walk through the valley of the shadow of death, [they] will fear no evil, for You are with [them], Your rod and Your staff, they comfort [them]" (Psalm 23:4). May they "Taste and see that the Lord is good; [and know that] blessed is the man who takes refuge in Him" (Psalm 34:8).

Comfort, carry, sustain, strengthen, encourage, and quiet the hearts of those who mourn, O Father of compassion and God of all comfort. Draw the brokenhearted to You.

Lord, show me specific and practical ways to serve those who mourn.

Day 25

Live in harmony with one another (Romans 12:16a).

Lord, make me a church member who causes my Pastor
very little trouble. Keep me from being a source of
contention, conflict, and strife. Strike envy and pride from
my heart and gossip from my lips. If I can't say something
encouraging, help me keep my mouth closed.

Help us to remember that we are family, and living
together as family always takes work. Convict us of the
need to "Make every effort to keep the unity of the Spirit
through the bond of peace" (Ephesians 4:3). Mature us so
that we choose to be obedient to Your Word and to Your
Spirit.

Help us apply Paul's words to our own lives. "Therefore, as God's chosen people, holy and dearly loved, clothe yourselves with compassion, kindness, humility, gentleness and patience. Bear with each other and forgive whatever grievances you may have against one another. Forgive as the Lord forgave you. And over all these virtues put on love, which binds them all together in perfect unity" (Colossians 3:12-14). To what degree do these virtues mark my life? What would it look like for me to literally "put on love"?

"Let the peace of Christ rule in your hearts, since as members of one body you were called to peace. And be thankful. Let the word of Christ dwell in you richly as you teach and admonish one another with all wisdom, and as you sing psalms, hymns and spiritual songs with gratitude in your hearts to God. And whatever you do, whether in word or deed, do it all in the name of the Lord Jesus, giving thanks to God the Father through Him" (Colossians 3:15-17). Lord, these verses pierce my heart. Show me how to respond in obedience.

"May the God who gives endurance and encouragement give [us] a spirit of unity amongst [ourselves] as [we] follow Christ Jesus, so that with one heart and mouth [we] may glorify the God and Father of our Lord Jesus Christ" (Romans 15:5-6). What must You do in me and in our church family, so that with one heart and mouth we glorify You?

Day 26

Do not be proud, but be willing to associate with people of low position. Do not be conceited (Romans 12:16b).

Here it is again – pride. O Lord, Your bringing forth water from the rock at Massah for the people of Israel was a marvelous work of Your power (Exodus 17:1-7). Strike and empty my heart of pride so that the waters of Your Spirit and love flow forth in my life. Make our church a place where oneness in Christ is a reality, no matter who we are or where we have been. There is no place for pride in this family.

Lord, You know my heart and its hidden places that no one else sees. I am ashamed to speak of it, but there are still pockets of self-righteousness and smugness there. They are like pockets of infection. Help me, O Healer. I cannot rid myself of this poison.

Day 27

Do not repay anyone evil for evil (Romans 12:17a).

We cannot wiggle around this one. When struck, we want to strike back. Lord, help us. "Let us fix our eyes on Jesus, the author and perfecter of our faith, Who for the joy set before Him endured the cross, scorning its shame, and sat down at the right hand of the throne of God. Consider Him Who endured such opposition from sinful men, so that you will not grow weary and lose heart" (Hebrews 12:2-3). O Jesus, show me what it means to fix my eyes on You.

Jesus, You are the author and perfecter of the faith. Strengthen me, when I am mistreated, to follow Your lead.

Day 28

Be careful to do what is right in the eyes of everybody (Romans 12:17b).

Cause us to be men and women, young people and children of integrity. May our behavior be above reproach. Mature us so that we make godly choices even when it goes against our own fleshly desires. Give us courage to do the right thing even when it goes against the tide of popular opinion.

Help us to "Be very careful, then, how [we] live – not as unwise but as wise, making the most of every opportunity, because the days are evil. Therefore do not be foolish, but understand what the Lord's will is" (Ephesians 5:15-16).

May we "…never tire of doing what is right" (2 Thessalonians 3:13). Let us not forget that Christ's honor is at stake in our bodily lives. O Holy Spirit, move in us and through us.

Day 29

If it is possible, as far as it depends on you, live at peace with everyone (Romans 12:18).

Let us "Make every effort to live in peace with all men and to be holy; without holiness no one will see the Lord" (Hebrews 12:14). What strained or broken relationships are there in my life today? What steps must I take in an effort to live at peace with these individuals?

_____

_____

_____

_____

_____

_____

_____

Make us peacemakers, not troublemakers.

_____

_____

_____

_____

_____

_____

_____

_____

_____

Guard our tongues. "Do not let any unwholesome talk come out of [my mouth] but only what is helpful for building others up according to their needs, that it may benefit those who listen" (Ephesians 4:29). Ouch! That one gets me every time.

_____

_____

_____

_____

_____

_____

_____

_____

_____

_____

"Let us therefore make every effort to do what leads to peace and to mutual edification" (Romans 14:19).

_____

_____

_____

_____

_____

_____

_____

_____

_____

_____

_____

_____

Day 30

Do not take revenge, my friends, but leave room for God's wrath, for it is written: 'It is mine to avenge; I will repay,' says the Lord. On the contrary: 'If your enemy is hungry, feed him; if he is thirsty, give him something to drink. In doing this, you will heap burning coals on his head.' Do not be overcome by evil, but overcome evil with good" (Romans 12:19-21).

O Sovereign Lord, our reputations, our relationships, and our very lives are in Your hands. Help us to trust You when enemies come against us.

Teach us that when wronged, we are to bring our disappointment and hurt to You. Listen to our cry. We pour out our hearts to You. In Your mercy and love, wipe away our tears and quiet our hearts.

_____

_____

_____

_____

_____

_____

_____

_____

_____

_____

_____

Help us to obey Your command to "Get rid of all bitterness, rage and anger, brawling and slander, along with every form of malice. Be kind and compassionate to one another, forgiving each other, just as in Christ God forgave you" (Ephesians 4:31-32).

_____

_____

_____

_____

_____

_____

_____

_____

Love is action. In what specific ways can I demonstrate love for my enemy, even when I do not feel like it?

My thoughts and prayers

My thoughts and prayers

My thoughts and prayers

My thoughts and prayers

My thoughts and prayers

Dear reader,

I thank my God for putting this book into your hands. If you already know Jesus Christ as your Lord and Savior, then you and I are family; we are one in Christ. "And this is my prayer: that your love may abound more and more in knowledge and depth of insight, so that you may be able to discern what is best ard may be pure and blameless until the day of Christ, filled with the fruit of righteousness that comes through Jesus Christ – to the glory and praise of God" (Philippians 1:9-11). May you live and love to His glory and praise!

Others may realize that a relationship is expressed in this book that you do not understand or share. Dear reader, are you one who feels that you are somehow on the outside looking in? Is the intimacy and love portrayed here something you long for? My prayer for you is that you will come to know Jesus as I am privileged to know Him. Jesus Christ is the Son of God. He came to earth and lived as a man, died on the cross, was raised from the dead, and ascended into heaven so that you and I might be forgiven of our sins and receive eternal life. Individuals who acknowledge their sin, turn from it, and receive Christ as their personal Lord and Savior are brought into an intimate and loving relationship with Him. When you receive Christ, you are born again as His Holy Spirit comes to live within you. By receiving Him, you are loved, forgiven, and free. You are now His child and a unique part of the body of Christ. Welcome to the family.

Christi Brown
El Paso, Texas

"Now to the King eternal,
immortal, invisible
the only God,
be honor and glory
for ever and ever. Amen."
1 Timothy 1:17

Scripture Index

Ephesians
1:6	38
3:18	39
4:3	99
4:12-13	42
4:22-24	26
4:29	110
4:31-32	112
4:32	60
5:1-2	59
5:15-16	108

Philippians
1:9-11	119
4:4	93
4:19	52

Colossians
3:12-14	100
3:15-17	101

1 Thessalonians
2:4b	54

2 Thessalonians
3:13	108

1 Timothy
1:17	121
6:11-12a	54
6:20a	54

2 Timothy
1:7	54
4:2	43

Titus
2:1	48
2:7b-8a	48
2:12-14	66

Philemon
6	29

Hebrews
6:10	46
4:15-16	81
12:2-3	105
12:14	109

James
3:17	56

1 Peter
4:11b	46
5:4	54

2 Peter
3:18	16

1 John
1:9	63
3:17-18	86